Living As God

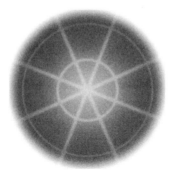

LIVING
AS GOD

HEALING *the* SEPARATION

REVISED EDITION

ROB McRAE

namaste
PUBLISHING

Vancouver, Canada

Library and Archives Canada Cataloguing in Publication

McRae, Rob, 1977-
   Living as God : healing the separation / Rob McRae. -- Rev. ed.

ISBN 978-1-897238-65-3

1. God. 2. Spiritual life. I. Title.

BT165.M37 2012   202'.117   C2012-901306-4

Published in the United States by
Namaste Publishing
P. O. Box 62084
Vancouver, British Columbia V6J 4A3
www.namastepublishing.com

Distributed in North America by PGW, Berkeley, CA USA
Typesetting by Steve Amarillo, Urban Design LLC

Printed and bound in the United States by Malloy Incorporated, Ann Arbor, MI

***All direct Bible quotes are taken from the King James Version,
unless noted otherwise.***

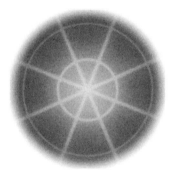

This book is dedicated to the one holding it now.

Yes, this is for you. You didn't come across these words by accident. Nothing ever happens by accident. What is occurring in your life right now is deliberate. The whole universe has conspired to create this moment exactly the way it is. Together, we have chosen to come to this page.

I have chosen it.

You have chosen it.

We have chosen it.

For all of life is connected; each breath and subtle movement influences all that is.

And together we are One.

How you choose to respond to this book influences the fate of the world. You are the only part of the collective whole who can alter the part of us that is you.

Your life is holy. This book has come to remind you of that. In fact, the whole universe exists to remind you of your true worth, to remind you that you are immeasurably more than a separate little person.

So I, a part of you, devote this book to you who are a part of me. This part of the One Self is dedicated to bringing forth whatever can help you more fully experience the joy and beauty of life.

This is your request.

This is your answer, sent forth with and from Love.

This book is dedicated to you—the One holding this Now.

1

As you read, you may arrive at the bottom of a page and realize that, although you have understood what is written, you cannot actually recall a single sentence. This is truly good news. It means that you are releasing the limitations of thought, of the thinking mind, and are being carried by the higher vibration of the heart that is embedded between these words and lines. This is the aim of all true teachers, whether they take the form of a human or a book. For any thought is useful only to the degree that it leads us into a deeper awareness through *feeling.* So do not rush through this work with a hungry mind. Let it sink in deeply. Let its feeling-tone linger in your energy. For the aim of this book is not to learn about God, but to dissolve preconceptions so we may realize what the word "God" truly means. When using the word God starts feeling futile, you know you are beginning to understand.

2

. . . .

"In the beginning was the Word, and the Word was with God, and the Word was God" (John 1:1). Then the Word was dispersed and made flesh, and could relate within Its Self. And in doing so, space and time were born. With space came distance. Separation was perceived. And with time, that separation was believed, and God became estranged within Its Self. The first Word, the One Word, had appeared to become the many, and the out breath was complete.

. . . .

The mystery of the first line of the Gospel of John has perplexed many for centuries. It has left readers of the Bible wondering, "What *is* this Word?" Yet at the time this gospel was written, its meaning was not obscure. The phrase "the Word" was borrowed from earlier, widely known Vedic texts, where it was often used as a direct substitute for their holiest of all words, the "Aum" or "Om," which is considered to be the word that represents all life. Translated into English, the word is notably similar: "Am," or more commonly, "I Am." The New Testament simply follows this tradition of substitution.

Therefore, whenever we see "the Word," we know that this implies the holy name of God: "I Am." So, in more modern language this earlier quotation reads, "In the beginning was the I Am, and the I Am was with God, and the I Am was God." The word *of* God, and the word *for* God, and the *name* of God are all the same thing— the I Am. I Am = God. The I Am *is* God. How many of us, however, pause to note and explore the obvious connection we have with this name of God?

One of our greatest human yearnings is our need to know God. This book is brought into manifestation by the collective call for help in this search. In our search, we must be ready to go beyond the word "God" and what we currently associate with it. This is the journey we are about to take. Words can still serve us in this journey, as long as we do not mistake these aids, these pointers to truth, for truth itself.

Once upon a time, when we had an inner certainty of the truth of our Being, we didn't need words for guidance. And may this be so again. Words offer a poor path to the reality of the ineffable, but for now, they are still one of the few tools for sharing ideas, feelings, and experiences related to the spiritual realm. Humankind has called this realm many things: the Tao, the Void, the Rigpa, God, Source. On and on go the words that are used in an attempt to express that which lies beyond words' limitations. The Infinite cannot be contained in a word any more than your essence can be conveyed by your name.

When it comes to words, the vast majority of humanity still associates a state of ultimate peace and fulfillment with the word "God." Consequently, this is the most highly charged of all words. It carries every confused vision, every misconception, yet every cherished hope of mankind.

How do we remove the encrusted, disfigured, outer shell of the word "God" so as to reveal its innermost truth? If we could fully convey the complete, indisputable truth of this one word, then in publishing it to the world, all seeking and suffering would cease. This is the dauntless challenge and intent of this book. If it is achieved in you, it will not be because of the words, but because of your readiness to feel the truth to which they point.

Awareness comes not through the thoughts that words evoke. Awareness is a *felt* experience that leaves a new, true, and permanent change in perception of reality. It's the mind that wants to reduce the ineffable to the confines of logical reasoning. The thinking mind separates out; it cannot appreciate true wholeness and thereby interferes with any experience of the divine and of God, which is the unity of all things.

We say God, Goddess, all that is, the Self, Consciousness, Energy, Being, Yahweh, Jehovah, Rigpa, I Am Presence, the Void, Isness, Oneness, Spirit, Tao, You, Me, Love, Light, Us, We, I, He, Her, It, One Self—and always these words point to God. Indeed, we are all synonymous; each of us has the same essential nature. If we understand one person or one thing fully we understand them all.

"God" is the word we use most often to describe all that we do *not* understand. It is also the word we use for all that we *do* understand. Yet once we think we understand something, we stop calling it God. We used to call a flash of light from the sky a sign of God, but now we know it simply as lightning. At one time, saving someone from dying of a poison would have been called a miracle. Now, with medical antidotes, we can achieve a quick chemical response to the poison, rendering it non-lethal to the body. The more we seem to understand, the less we need to ascribe to God. From this perspective, God has become increasingly narrow in some people's minds. However, when we start to sense the Spirit of all things—the essence behind each form—we find that the word "God" expands again to encompass everything.

For centuries most of humanity has held an extremely dysfunctional image of an outside, anthropomorphic God, which has severely limited the human race in all its endeavors and been the cause of much suffering. In order for us to break free, to evolve, this conditioned, misleading view must be dropped. Yes, we could try to simply avoid the word "God" in our philosophical dialogues and spiritual pursuits, yet eventually it must be integrated for our own inner healing. We can talk about Universal Life Force or the Universal Mind, but eventually we will ask, "But how does all of this relate to God?" This is the fundamental question.

A requisite part of this inquiry is how do *you* relate to God? When you close your eyes and say the word "God," what images, thoughts, and feelings emerge? What does God mean for *you*? Do you feel anger toward God, fearful of Him, or do you feel ambivalent and unsure of what this charged word could be? Are you an agnostic or an atheist? Do you feel love towards Her, or do you feel neglected?

Regardless of your response, we all have a relationship to this word and to this force that must be explored, for the path to inner peace spirals through its essence.

Life, God, extends Itself through you. This is our individual and collective purpose—to give expression to God, to be the Living God. And this includes you. Through our existence God can look on Its Self and see Its beauty.

s God outside of you, inside of you, or all around you? Is God a person or a power? A fantasy or a reality? God may mean ultimate power for you. God may be a name for nothingness, as in some Buddhist texts. God is represented by a single man for some Christians, every man for the Hindus, silence for the Taoists, and sound to the Vedic seers. God evokes a state of peace to some, and to others God is a legitimate reason for war. God has been described as a powerful lion of a creator and also as meek as a lamb. For some, planet Earth is God, and everything *but* the physical realm is God for many new age thinkers. The Tantrists find God through sex, yet Catholic priests seek God through chastity. Why such confusion? Why such disagreement?

In truth, all are correct. God is without opposite or opposition. Virtually by definition God is everything, always—the beginning and the end, infinite and omnipresent. *There can be nothing that is not God.* How could anything be in conflict with the power that creates life and moves through it always? If God truly exists, it is as the essence of everything that is—without exception. Really, "God" is just a word that we use to point to that essence which is nowhere not present. Not for any reason. Not ever.

Does this change the meaning of the word "God" for you? If so, this is a very good thing!

It has been over 2000 years since Jesus walked the earth, preaching the kingdom of heaven within. Since then, His words, the word "God," and the word *of* God have been altered significantly. We are ready now for an evolutionary leap in consciousness, which will bring clarity to all spiritual teachings. It is time to redeem the words of God. For this is the purpose of the Christ—to bring God to life in the hearts of all men. This has been the mission of every true spiritual master—to make God live again among men, to resurrect man's Holy Spirit to breathe the life of remembrance into our consciousness. In order to do this, it is necessary to reject any part of your self that feels in essence different from and potentially less than the man known as Jesus. This is true for any spiritual guide you look up to, be it Jesus, Buddha, Mohammed, Archangel Michael, or Saint Germain. Although this may be against the teachings of established Christian religions, it is a glorious irony that it is exactly what Jesus Himself taught: "The works that I do shall he do also; and greater works than these shall he do" (John 14:12).

Do not believe that you will only do these things when you get to heaven, for He also told us in Matthew that the kingdom of heaven is here and now. It is indeed ironic that what some would have us believe is the greatest sin is, in fact, not sin at all but a sign—a sign that we are remembering the truth: we and God are One.

We have come here to remember—I Am that "I Am." The great teachings implore us to "Know thy self." They also tell us to "Know thy God." However, most important, they tell us that to know thy self *is* to know God. Although we may perceive this to be most radical, it is truly the most primal of spiritual teachings. This message has never changed, nor will it ever. Humanity's acceptance of it is the only thing to ever shift.

Jesus understood clearly the connection between himself and the Father. This is the source of his power and influence on the world. He had power because he lived in constant awareness of and alignment with his oneness with divine Source. To worship Jesus the man or any other spiritual master or prophet is to gravely miss the mark. Do not worship their physical form or worship them for their works; recognize instead the very same glory residing in your own self. That is what the Buddha taught us to do. That is what Jesus taught us was possible. Yet their teachings have been skewed and clouded. This is why we are now calling forth other aspects of the One Self—to express again the eternal truth for which we thirst. This book comes to remind you that you, as part of the One Self, are God.

To help you understand who you are, consider the following analogy:

The sunlight that floods your room is of course made up of countless individual rays. All of these rays are expressions of the sun in the sky. They have no existence other than the sun since they are emanations of the sun. And yet the sun is also so much more. So we could say that the sun and its rays are one.

Similarly, we are each expressions of God. Like the sun rays are the sun's expression, each of us is God's expression. As the sun rays are one with the Sun, so too we as individuals are one with God. Collectively, we are sunlight.

3

Let me introduce you to God.

He is right here, standing with you. She is right now hearing you, feeling you. God is always with us, as we've been told. So where is She? Why can't we experience Him for ourselves? Simply because we do not recognize God.

Do you really even know your self? Go now, and look in the mirror. Look behind the familiar form. Do you see who is looking back at you from behind those beautiful eyes? This is the God you do not recognize, for It looks surprisingly just like you! Now go and look at a neighbor. Do you see who is looking back at you from behind those beautiful eyes? This is the God you do not recognize, for It looks surprisingly just like your neighbor.

Both of you, and everything that is, are united as a single field of consciousness. Simultaneously, we are also dispersed into many points of experience where our name could be Peter or Jesus or Maryanne. If we have forgotten this, it is all right. We have allowed ourselves to forget. However, we can also allow ourselves to remember. It's that simple.

In essence, you are God. This is the obvious truth we do not hear, clearly expressed and demonstrated by masters we have ignored. God, being love, extends Itself naturally to create all that is. This is the great insight we prevent our selves from having, going as far as creating institutions and religions to keep us from seeing it. Why? Because to accept this truth would mean the death of all we have been conditioned to believe. It would mean the end of our current perception of who we have come to see our selves as—separate, vulnerable, limited persons needing to struggle and defend ourselves against "others." There would be no more conflict, no more aggression, no more drama, no more unease, displeasure, or even disease if we were to accept our Oneness. To the ego, to the falsely-created self that is based on separation from others, this means its death. And this is why people tend to unconsciously resist the purest spiritual teachings that have been with us for centuries: they do not serve the needs or goals of the egoic self.

The full realization of the One Self is indeed a death. It is the death of that separate, projected self that most people believe to be their whole being. It is this belief in separation that prevents their spiritual awakening.

Jesus said it clearly: "Ye are gods" (John 10:34). What did we think he was saying? We have managed to reject this, to misinterpret this simple phrase in so many ways. But like most of His sayings, it is powerful because it is clear and to the point. We just don't want to hear it.

You are God. This is the difficult proclamation, the mystery, and the koan of this age. It is true, and it is also not true. It depends on what you mean by *you*, and what you mean by *God*.

The saying is true if what you mean by *you* has very little to do with your body, your name, your person, but rather the essence of life within. And if by *God* you mean the ground of being that abides in all things—then again this saying is true.

If, however, "You are God" is taken to mean that you are a separate individual with spiritual power who is somehow equal to the historical, projected image of an almighty creator, then this is a disastrous misinterpretation.

Thought and mind create this world like the film in a projector creates the movie on the screen. Yet our great spiritual destiny is not to merely create better movies, but to realize that we are neither the characters nor the story, but the light that illumines the projector, carries all images, and upon which the whole charade must rest.

This realization is our great awakening, our deep healing, our peace.

Chasing abundance is a great spiritual path only because at some point the emptiness of the world will become totally clear. Then, you will look entirely beyond the form, and inside the emptiness you may find the fullness of your real essence. And if you look with sincerity, you will see that it is all you need—it is divinity itself.

4

Who am I? This is the most natural and fundamental of all inquiries. God already answered when asked this question. She responded, "I Am that I Am." And we questioned God's answer. "What does this mean?" we wondered. "What is this I Am?" "Who is this I Am?" We tried to give *form* to the answer.

"Who am I?" Always, we come back to the same question. But who are we really asking? Ourselves? God? More importantly, who is it who responds? Always, this question has been in the first person. Who Am I? I Am that I Am. This question and this answer are always the same—regardless of who is asking it, regardless of who is responding to it. It is no different for one person than it is for another. The question and answer will be the same whether we ask God, whether we ask another being, or even if God asks us. But this still leaves us wondering: Who are You, God? This is what we *really* want to know.

We say we are soul searching, that we are trying to find our self, and that we are looking for God. Yet these all involve the same process—the inquiry into the nature of our Source. Discovering this Source is what great saints identify as the purpose of life. Different descriptions of and approaches to finding the purpose of life fill many books. One Eastern spiritual tradition simply and clearly calls the paths and the goal "self-realization."

It is significant that past and current spiritual masters tell us that to know thy self is also to know God. However, this has been difficult for us to comprehend. How can it be that we are one and the same? And if we are, what does this *really* mean? This is what we are here to clarify: Who and what is the I Am?

L isten.

I Am in the silence between these words and lines, and underneath the very air you breathe. What I Am and who you are, are the same. We share our essential beingness. Every heart beats with the same life force. This is the miracle and mystery of life. Let us explore our essence so we may come to the *felt* realization that though you and I are different persons, beyond this—in our spirit—we are one.

"*Me*" *is not the One who is great. It is the One Spirit, as me, who is great.*

It is an immense error to believe that *I* could possibly be better than *you.* Indeed, this is truly impossible. At the level of essence, at the spiritual level, we are all equal. For this reason, all self-realized beings are very humble. If you feel in any way that you are greater than or less than another, this is a sure indication that you are not seeing with correct vision. You are not seeing with the eyes of the Soul.

You were divine when you were born, when you were growing up, and are divine still. You don't have to *become* holy. You already are. You need only *accept* your holiness. See beyond your seeming imperfections to your perfection. See your divinity even when it is not evident in worldly terms. In fact, see divinity *especially* when it is not visible in worldly terms. See the mundane as miraculous. For it is. Do not wait for a special teacher, a church, a special meditation, or a lakeside retreat. Being fully present while tending to our garden, waiting for the car to be fixed, or buying groceries—it is in simple moments like these that we experience our divinity.

Don't seek yourself outside of yourself. Don't be so eager to be spiritual that you leave your humanity behind. They are the same. Evolution does not mean giving up human experience in favor of spiritual experience, but means shifting your perception to recognize that the human experience *is* spiritual.

It is of little benefit merely to repeat to ourselves that Krishna lives in every heart, that Buddha is alive in everything, that the Tao flows with and through all things. Each time we do we point to the same truth, but do we truly grasp it? There is enormous resistance in the human psyche to the idea of our divinity. It can bring great fear, for it changes everything.

We have said that we need and desire great changes in our world. For the first time in human history there appear to be enough individuals who have the readiness and level of awareness to make these changes. These individuals know that we cannot change just a little bit. We must be transformed. And our transformation occurs through complete acceptance of and surrender to the Spirit in and behind all things.

Pride is the trademark of the ego. Humility is the trademark of the soul. We can't claim to personally own or accomplish anything as a separate person since all comes from the same source. This is the realization of the master and why the master is so humble. Therefore, bring humility to all that you do. For humility vanquishes the ego. It dissolves all boundaries. No simple passivity or modesty will do. It must be true humility, which occurs when you psychologically let go of everything you used to think of as your own: ideas, possessions, desires, fears—all attachments are surrendered to the all-inclusiveness of the One. You recognize that all is embodied in the One, the I Am Presence that is All. Releasing pride involves understanding that your personal identity is nothing more than a façade, and that you are Divine Presence. Because of this, there is nothing to work toward or try to hold onto since you are all and embody all. This is why it is not I but the Father who does these things. In God consciousness there is no isolation or comparison. And this is why we judge not. Everything is shared; nothing is hidden since there is nothing that needs to be protected through pretense.

To quickly experience humility, you may want to go do something the mind finds typically embarrassing, and instead of letting it make you shrink and feel inferior, laugh at its inability to touch your true self. Expand into the experience. Next, go and do something grand, magnanimous—anything to try to make yourself look better or stand out from another. Then remind yourself that all of your personal efforts to be morally superior, stronger than, better than others, are also in vain. What you think about yourself or what anyone else *thinks* about you could never increase or decrease your true worth.

It is no mistake that you have humble roots. How else can you meet others on common ground? Your past, filled with mistakes, does not negate your divinity, but rather enhances your understanding of and compassion for others, and makes you and others more mutually accessible. So do not be hard on yourself for being human. Rather, recognize that being human is a means to embody your divinity.

What could anyone else do that makes him or her more than you are? What could you ever do to make yourself one bit better than your neighbor? In our efforts to be better than we already are and better than others, we only prove how completely we have forgotten something important: we can go beyond nobody. We can only go beyond identifying our selves solely with the physical body, which is a mistaken belief that needs to be transcended. Identifying solely with our body leads us to believe we are separate. When we let go of all the conditioned mind patterns that speak of separation—of things we need to survive, to succeed, to be happy, to be loved— then the self is finally able to reunite with primal reality. This basic reality to which we return when we release the ego and its ways is the reality in which we are God.

Not *a* god.

The God.

There is only one God, and it is the Oneness.

That One Being lives through every body.

We believe we need to grow in consciousness and become more spiritual to become divine. This is false, and it only gives evidence for and reinforces our belief that we are separate from the greater, spiritual Self. Our superficial layer of self—the ego—is what prevents us from experiencing our true nature. The limited self-image created by the ego is what needs to dissolve for the One Presence to be experienced. And this is *all* that needs to happen.

dentification with the egoic self keeps you from God. A wise soul once said, "God equals man minus ego." He who is least in ego is most in Spirit. Even if you accept this, you are likely afraid to give up your sense of self. You see the egoic mind's dissolution as your death since you have been living with the belief that the false egoic self is who you are. Be at peace, though. Death of your true self is impossible. That death cannot come. You cannot lose your true self; you can only gain remembrance of it. Then you find that what you thought was your self holds but a tiny shred of your magnificence.

Who you think you are, and your efforts to maintain and enhance this, are exactly what keep you from experiencing what you really are—which is already perfect and complete.

If a hand reaching out of the clouds or a person materializing objects out of thin air were truly the most useful triggers for our self-realization, then surely we would see more of this. However, they are not. These only reinforce our sense of separation. If a man in white robes appeared from out of the sky to teach us about inner holiness, we might pay attention to his teaching but would end up worshipping him as separate from ourselves. A better way for Spirit to bring peace to earth is for a messenger to grow up in our world as a child, to live as an ordinary human, to blossom into self-realization, and to be an example for others. This is why we have you. This is your spiritual purpose.

Separation is not inherent in life. It is a figment of the mind. Perception is the only basis for division in the world. How you perceive your world is how you will receive your world. Your ability to adjust your perception of the world is how you can experience a different reality. If you choose to see unity through the eyes of unconditional love, then fear and its barriers will dissolve.

Remember that you, Jesus, the Buddha, Mohammed, and all beings and things are but different points of focus we hold in our Oneness. You are as much a part of them as you choose to see, and likewise, they are a part of you. The national hero is just another of the infinite number of lives that you are living as the great One Self that I Am. There are beings whose energy is akin to yours, but essentially every life is one of your own. Each one influences you, just as you influence it. Your brother Don is one aspect of your self, your neighbor is another of your lives as Spirit, and every person who has or will live is but another focus, perspective, and expression of the Oneness that I Am.

The only significant difference between you and Jesus, between you and the Buddha, is that they remembered who they are.

The perception of separation from God occurs as soon as there is the slightest notion of time and space. With the belief in time and space comes distance, which separates one from another. When we see ourselves as separate beings, the concept of being more or less appears, and this is where fear and need are born. We cannot return to God because we never left God. We only had a *thought* that we did.

Separation between you and God is as real as you think it is. Being one with God involves a correction of perception, not an attempt to return to God. Paradoxically, our effort to move back into God reinforces the illusion of separation (God is there, I am here). You cannot move in time and space *back into* God. You can only realize that you are already there.

Why would we want to believe in the illusion of separation if we are already One? As God we know we are absolutely safe, that all is well. Perhaps we chose to see ourselves as split from our One Self in playful curiosity to find out what it would be like to not feel like we were God. Perhaps we chose to see ourselves as separate simply to have the experience of joyfully reuniting in Oneness again. Could it be that the sweetness of that embrace is so compelling we create the pain of believed separation just so we can experience the elation of atonement? Have we chosen all the bumps we experience in life simply to make our reunion even more glorious? Perhaps we chose to experience this world with its pain so we could grow in wisdom and compassion not possible if we never forgot our unity. Perhaps in the infinite wisdom of the One, we left home in order to experience again what home truly is. The irony is that we return by remembering that we never could, nor did we ever, leave our home in God in the first place.

The egoic self craves security, yet the heart insists that moving forward is the only way to real freedom. It is indeed ironic that, while we claim we want spiritual enlightenment, we are unwilling to part with our identification with name and form. It is only the insistence of holding on to this that prevents us from experiencing God. This is what the dramatic tragedies seek to teach us: after the ego has its way—after pride—cometh the fall. To prevent tragedy, relinquish the ego. Surrender to the benevolence of the Oneness. Let pride fall so it does not fell you. This ends the human drama—our fictional "stories" born out of perceived separation.

It can be exciting to act out our egoic roles, but many of us have finally had enough. We can choose to stop pretending that we are other than the embodied presence of the One. It is our choice— about who we are.

End of story.

Beginning of peace.

Within the Oneness, there is no other. The entire cosmos is encoded in every atom. Every reality is a hologram. The microcosm *is* the macrocosm. As above, so below. On earth, as it is in heaven. You contain the whole of life's infinite presence. Your neighbor is part of you, just as is a rock on Mars or the thought of a being light years away. Everything you do, say, or think affects the energies around you and thereby the potential realities of the whole universe. The way a farmer in Thailand chops his food creates a wave in the cosmos that ripples through you as you drive to work.

Be aware that what you keep in your mind does truly change the world. For the way you drive to work influences the way a farmer in Thailand chops his food. Modern physicists refer to this as the "Butterfly Effect" and tell us of the indisputable evidence of non-local cause. This confirms our true connection.

Heaven is the experiencing of the One. The portal to it is without door. It is wide enough for all sentient beings to pour through at once. No one is barred; those who do not enter have chosen not to. It is not found after death, nor through some work or more time. Unity is available now. Indeed, it is *only* available right now. It is a decision for complete love.

Psychics and those who channel are not more gifted than you. They have just experienced that they can tune into different aspects of the One Self, much like we choose to tune into different radio frequencies to hear different programs. Common intuition, novel creations, and breakthrough insights result from nothing other than tapping into the greater intelligence of the One Self. It is for this reason that artists of all kinds, inventors, and the like of Einstein acknowledge a higher "force" at work in what they do or come to see. Synchronicities result from our connection and agreement with other parts of our One Self that influence our denser human plane. See if the more you open to the One Self the more you experience these so-called coincidences.

5

We are all different beams of the same light—shining into each other, shining through each other. We are all different ways that the same Holy Presence is living and experiencing its one, common light.

To speak of your inequity, of your obvious sin, of the karma you need to work out, is to gravely misperceive. To awaken spiritually is to see the perfection that you already are. Spiritual mastery does not require years of arduous spiritual practice. It takes a moment of sincerity. Mastery is simple. It requires only that you live as if all were one. No principle, code, or set of rules is of any value unless it helps you do this. So, live according to this One rule; then, only the One shall rule.

Every *true* law, doctrine, religious command, moral or philosophical principle, is but an extension of the rule of One— *that we are all One as Source.* Perceiving life as filled with complexity and problems, we have missed this simple truth, this short answer. Such is the way of mathematics as well: deeply complex, intricate problems may yield a single digit answer. And so it is also with the mystery of life. The answer, clear and true, underlying all the complexity of life is really just a single number: One. Oneness. We can choose to go through the process of arduous problem-solving, arduous searching, or accept this truth right now. It is our choice. Only we decide how difficult or easy it will be.

We are one.
Life is one.
Me + you + every other one + everything = God.
Me + you + every other one + everything + God = One.

There is nothing else to figure out. Any other answer is but a step, a fraction on its way to this eventual simplification.

You can choose to abandon your life of seeming complex problems by seeing there are no true problems, just a solution. This solution dissolves all fears, all guilt, all effort. Like the drop of water realizing it is the ocean, we are invited to see ourselves, not as being isolated, but as part of all that is. When we realize the essence of this sea, that all the glory and power of life is already within us, we will be washed clean of multiplicity and personal struggle.

M astery or enlightenment are deceptive words because they carry the notion that we must become more holy in order to be aligned with the One. Godliness, however, may very well entail fetching wood and carrying water. It may also be checking out groceries eight hours a day. Every true spiritual master bows to you just as steeply as you do before them, for they see the divine light in you, too. In truth, you cannot accept your own divine light without acknowledging it in another.

You will know a master because he is at one with his fellow man. It is true that some holy persons have demonstrated immense power and abundance on earth, but there have also been fully realized souls who have lived in apparent poverty. Both are meant to show us that things are not always as they appear. To worship a spiritual master as apart from and more worthy than you is idolatry. Those beings are no greater than you. They, like each of us, are simply other facets of the One Self. Mother Mary lives within you. Archangel Michael is an expression of us and so is the stranger on the street. Even the terrorist lives within you.

All is One as God.

God is the source of and the sum of all life.

God is the part and the whole.

God is the perfect harmony of all.

And always, God is Love. To live in love with the world is to live as God.

Be Love; be God.

Be compassionate, patient, and accepting of your self and others.

Be good to each other.

Be God to each other.

The way to achieve spiritual enlightenment is not complex, obscure, or mysterious. Time, special gifts, or difficult practices are not required to achieve it, nor a handbook, a knowledge of metaphysics, or adherence to a particular religious belief system. You need only think as if we all are One. Or more precisely, stop thinking we are two. Take away all multiplicity, and what is left is the One. The path to Love is not steep and long. It is not a huge leap of faith. It is just a single step forward in your perception.

For the way is truly straight and narrow.

Indeed, it can accommodate only One.

It fits only the Oneness.

So if your focus is on the One, you shall be it.

If thine eye be single, then thine "I" shall be One. "The light of the body is in the eye. If therefore thine eye be single, then thy whole body shall be full of light" (Matthew 6:22).

Every person and every form is but an idea in the mind of God. Each person originates from Spirit as consciousness. Consciousness begets energy. Energy begets thought. Thought takes form. Although we perceive our bodies to be separate from one another, we are all just different forms projected from the same universal consciousness. Because of this, we are not static, not inflexible person-boxes, but can change by changing our own thoughts.

Who we think we are right now is one tiny idea in our collective mind. The only fixed and common point of our individual and collective being is Spirit, which is evidenced as *consciousness itself.* Everything else that we are will change. All forms change. But the I Am remains. Beyond this constant, we can think and therefore be anything we dream of being. It is only our thoughts that can ever hold us back.

Our external life is simply the sum of our thoughts. If you thought exactly like the Buddha, you would be the Buddha. If you thought exactly like Jesus, you would be Jesus. Of course, you can't, literally, but at least in theory this is true. Because we are all a part of everyone and everything, all is always available to us through the attraction of our thoughts. If you spent your whole life studying and imitating the thoughts of another person, you would eventually embody much of their energy. It doesn't require a lifetime for that to happen. Indeed, it happens to some degree with every person you agree with, make friends with, or that you influence. For it is not our bodies that keep us separate from each other, but our thoughts.

We define ourselves by the thoughts we keep. Those we don't identify with we leave behind. By either adopting or disowning thoughts we establish how we will experience ourselves. Your experience of yourself is a compilation of ideas that shifts every day according to your choices. You can confirm this by noting your self-image from one day to another.

Who you think you are can be a very limited concept based upon those ideas you *currently* adhere to. When you change your ideas of who you are, you become a different person. In another moment, a week, or 60 years from now there could be an altogether different set of ideas called "you." But there is an essence behind all these thoughts that remains the same. It is here in this moment, and it existed before you were born, and will continue after this set of thoughts called "you" dies. What is that essence? Try to get in touch with it, and you may see that it is present in all things.

This is not hard to understand. However, if we apply this to the present, we can see that right now we are simultaneously alive in every single other person who exists. For each being is but another idea expressed by our One Self. Let us remember this the next time we are quick to judge another. For all we know, they could be our past or future self. Which aspect of your self do you think has written this book? Is it your past, your present, or your future?

It is your history, if you feel beyond it.
It is your future, if you feel behind it.
It is your present, if you accept it.

6

What do you want in life? And who or what do you suppose is giving or not giving it to you? More than anything, don't we want to be free of "need"—mental, emotional, physical, spiritual? When we are not needy, we are free to fully partake in the joy of life; we are more easily able to be completely present and respond according to the need of the moment.

If you knew you already had everything because you *are* already everything, would you not act differently than you do now? Would you worry about tomorrow? Would you still be afraid to trust your brother? Who could be an enemy?

If you accept that God is omnipresent then you must accept that you are one with God simply because you exist. That means you are also one with all life. And in this unity there is no lack. The reality of your spirit means you could never go without. You do not need–in your oneness all is available to you.

In truth, to live is to create. There is never a time when we are not creating. The energetic blueprint of every thought, emotion, action, and breath we emit returns to us in kind. What if we lived this awareness each moment? Would we not be empowered? Would we not carefully choose our thoughts, feelings, and actions?

Most of us are unconscious of our creative nature. When we live unconsciously, most of what we experience is repetitious. It comes from our conditioned past and our habits. It is no wonder that we notice repetitive patterns in our lives.

Choose to love, and watch how peace follows. Choose to worry, and see how it brings pain. Each moment holds infinite possibilities and only awaits your call into experience. It is of lesser importance *what* you choose than that you are aware you have a choice–not necessarily in what you will experience, but always in how you respond to it.

In circumstance you can be rich or poor, but what do you want within? If you want an abundance of objects and experiences in this life you may or may not get them. But if you want peace, compassion, connection to the divine—these things you can have no matter what. They do not depend on circumstance. They depend only on your choice to have them.

So never mind the religion of abundance and the creation of prosperity. Create humility. Manifest inner calm. Succeed in forgiveness. The external life will follow in kind, like the apple blossom on the apple tree. It is the seeds we sew which require our attention. The fruits will come on their own.

As individuals we each create, but only as a single expression of the collective in communion with the whole.

We are all part of the cosmic author. On the level of spirit, the universe is like a story whose beginning and ending, and everything in between, is already known. However, to the person, to the human that you think you are, it is all fresh and new. It may be truer to see the cosmos like a movie with an infinite number of plots, like a choose-your-own-adventure book, where *every* possible choice, in every fraction of a moment, is somehow played out.

Every character is still essentially an expression of the author's mind. And the author is still just One Self. It can and does experience any life, and indeed, every life. The author can change things, it can look at any level and possibility. In our deepest self, we are that author.

If we could remember this, we would begin to relax a little and trust whatever is. It is all already written.

Now, the question is: do you want to continue to be lost in the drama, or can you fall into the silence, read between the lines of life, and connect to a deeper essence?

Once our story is over, we can decide to experience it again, edit it, switch roles, and add different sub-plots, keeping the theme but developing different potentials each time, delighting in re-experiencing the endless possibilities and facets of our One Self. We can do this again and again. In fact, we do. We do it until we have had enough and we are ready for peace.

Drama carries an addictive charge that temporarily gives us a false sense of aliveness. But if we want peace and lasting joy, we must look past all of this—past the words, past the names and forms, past the story, and see the Source behind it all.

A plan of creation is not set in stone. It is just that—a plan to create, a decision to freely experience endless possibilities. The current human need for security cannot be found in the world of form, for the physical world is not static. As it has been said: the only constant is change.

So take no thought for tomorrow. If you feel you *must* plan, plan for the unexpected, for the universe will be a different place tomorrow— and so will you. Change is built into the very act of creating. The cosmos is created by thought, and I Am the thinker.

7

The mind asks, "Well, how can all of us be creators? Wouldn't this mean conflict, competition, chaos? How can each of us be gods? Spirit answers: "We are not all gods. We are all God. There cannot be more than one God."

Since there is only one Self, any facet can only act with the agreement and support of the rest. Within the One Self, there is only complete agreement, complete harmony. In this way, we see that our personal choices *must* be the perfect will of God, that our choices *are* God's choices.

I t is easy to say that since you are creative, you have made every thing that is in your life. But what part of you created that surprise inheritance or sudden disease? Creation–just like you–is multi-dimensional. Your conscious thoughts create only a small percentage of what actually occurs in life. Your greater soul, your spirit that is connected on universal levels, is the source of most of your life, of which your mind is not aware. So let go of the guilt and the burden. Trust that every event in life comes from a level of your self that is giving you exactly what you need, in every moment. Instead of trying to control and force results, try to look at how the results are inviting you into a more profound experience of life. Whatever is about you, right now, exists for a sacred purpose—to somehow give you an opportunity to more fully embrace the divine. Look then for a way to do this, and fulfill the purpose of your day.

The subconscious level of self, like the rest, also plays a part in the creation of our lives. It is often a repository for all that we could not consciously handle at the time. This includes mainly our fears, which continue to exist until we are able to embrace them at the conscious level. We *can* choose, however, to bring consciousness to the fear as it surfaces and reveals itself in the present. This is the gift of the failed relationship, the loss of the job, or of an unexpected illness—it stirs up old, repressed negativity so we can finally deal with it. When we do this, when we face our fear and hold it in the truth of our life as it exists *now*, we will almost always see that the fear is no longer valid, that it is based on some very old hurt.

This is the moment of the gift—when we can say, "Yes, there is an unpleasant, painful feeling which comes from a fear I choose to no longer believe in." We may then have the strength to laugh at our fears, which is an act of such love that any darkness is washed away and all hidden faces become clear. This conscious moment is the light that dissolves limitation. This is how we reclaim our lives.

Eventually, when we are able to sustain a constant awareness of our true selves, there will be no more hidden thoughts, no more psychological fear, no more subconscious mind. Then, even the super-conscious, which in this context is the unlimited, all-knowing mind of the One Self, ceases to be separate. This is what it means to be a fully realized being: all aspects of self are integrated, whole, united.

In the grander scheme, everything, regardless of the imperfections we seem to be creating, is just perfect. Within the One Self, everything finds agreement and is honored and celebrated. Keep this in mind the next time you try to fix someone's life. You are not responsible for creating another person's reality, so why carry the burden of trying to do so? The best you can do is be an example of what it is like to know the One Self. They will see that you need nothing from them, and they may then learn to need nothing from you. And then all of us may learn that we need nothing, least of all from a source external to our selves. It is all already here within us. Writer and Unity Minister Eric Butterworth saw this clearly when he said, "We do not pray *to* God, we pray *from* the consciousness *of* God."[1]

[1] Butterworth, Eric, *The Creative Life* (Jeremy P. Tarcher/Penguin, New York, NY 2001), 9

8

Being everything, you see that all you desire to attain, achieve, or acquire is already within you. You simply need to call it forth into your life. Everything is possible for those who know that all possibilities exist within them.

You can select your very next moment from infinite possibilities. This is true for everyone. It is why role models—among them spiritual masters—are so important. They provide examples of different ways of being. This is why we look to them—to show us a way to be as they are, to experience what they experience. This is why we are so interested in knowing the thoughts of those we admire—to see the connection between what they think, what they experience, and what they do. Intuitively, we know there is a causal relationship between them.

What you observe as the outer life of another is but their perceptions of their world in action—the projection of their thoughts. This is what your life is too—the experience born of the sum and characteristic energies of all your thoughts. This is why if you want to become the best athlete you can be, have the necessary physical capability, and have the opportunity to observe a master of the sport, do not study only the details of their personal and training habits. For even if you were to copy their habits exactly, you may only end up injured. Their athletic accomplishments are not brought about primarily by their practices, but by their perspective. If you could also imitate exactly how they think and their intuitive "knowing," you would be able to imitate their success.

Whatever you want to do, find someone who exemplifies it, and take your cue from their life.

It is easy to understand why spiritual seekers value the presence and teachings of a spiritual master. Jesus remains one of the great masters. Hindus, Buddhists, Muslims, and many others agree that He gave us an extraordinary example to live by. He came to earth to demonstrate a particular way of life. He saw that even though the world of flesh can be dark and corrupt, although suffering was widespread and belief in separation ever present, in essence all of us are divine. We are of the same source; we have the same "Father." Jesus saw his own genuine, immutable holiness, and he saw the same Self in all of us—man, woman, leper, pauper, prostitute, and priest.

To be like Jesus, we must learn to see the world in a similar way. Read his words. Feel their essence. He allowed his mind to open to and merge with the cosmic mind. He embodied God on earth, so "Let this mind be in you, which was also in Christ Jesus" (Philippians 2:5).

This is not only possible but also inevitable. We cannot help but embody God. We are already the fullness of the Creator. It is our destiny to realize this. If we do not experience this, it is because we have severed ourselves from unconditionally loving ourselves and those around us. The moment this feeling is recaptured, simultaneously we experience the presence of God—as us. For love is the only thought of God. This is why *A Course In Miracles* tells us,

"Teach only love, for that is what you are."[2] This is what we have been practicing to do all of our life times—to be love, to be divine presence. God, the expression of unconditional love, is our supreme role model.

Our spiritual journey is toward God, toward our Source. We all are striving to be like God. This is not blasphemous or egotistical, but honest. It is evidence that we want to remember.

Even the ego wants to be like God. However, because it sees its source as a separate, powerful creator, it shapes itself accordingly. And so we see individuals being driven by greed, defensiveness, and the need to control.

Everything aligns with Source through its perceived relationship with Source. Wherever you feel you have come from, this is the direction in which you are heading. If you believe you come from a wrathful, judgmental God separate from yourself, you will become a source of fear to yourself and to others. If you feel you are simply the product of your biological parents, you are destined to live much the same way they did. If you believe you have been born of blissful love, this is what you will grow into.

This is why our relationship with our parents is of such importance in understanding life. It is a clear, human model of our relationship with our source. During our formative years, we see our parents as being our Source and define ourselves through the quality of our relationship with them. When we grow up and redefine our Source as being of a spiritual nature, we must heal any discord we feel toward our parents, lest it taint the way we relate to the world.

[2] *A Course in Miracles* (Foundation for Inner Peace, Glen Allen, California 1990) Text, Chapter 6, 87

I t is not only our parents to whom we give power to shape our lives. Any time we give another person or situation the responsibility for creating part of our life experience, we unconsciously accept them to be our source. Our energy then inevitably aligns with their energy and the qualities they embody. So if there is any person or situation you feel is creating your world for you, examine how you see them, for this is what you are in the process of becoming. This is why it is essential that you see no other way to the Source save through your self. No one comes to the Father, except through the I Am. For a way that is not through your own self leads to a false source, not to your true spiritual home. Our relationship to Source is, in essence, eternal and unchanging. However, how we *perceive* our connection to our source can change; then our energetic association with it shifts accordingly. Where do you think you came from? Were you born in original sin or in creative ecstasy? Are you a victim of circumstance, life's impartial participant, or its creator? Your beliefs color every aspect of your life.

9

"Be ye therefore perfect, even as your Father which is in heaven is perfect" (Matthew 5:48). Perfection is not a flawless state, a state when one ceases to make "mistakes," but a natural state of the soul where one has transcended the need to judge seeming flaws and faults. Unconditional love and acceptance allow us to see this perfection beyond the duality of good and bad. Only when we believe in separation can we imagine things to be wrong as they are, which inevitably leads to fear, desire, and suffering of all kinds. Believing in separation from the One Self, we produce on-going cycles of individual and collective winners and losers, victims and perpetrators.

When we are told to live with unconditional love, this invites us to drop all criticism of what lies before us—to see only perfection. The divine One Self sees all as perfect, since it sees with the eyes of unconditional acceptance and love.

Do you love your life as it is? This is not easy; the human mind has developed many stipulations on what it takes for life to be good enough. But nothing less than perfect will do, since we know in our hearts perfection is our natural state. Joy and peace are more than a right, they are the stuff we are made of. Yet our conditioned beliefs keep us from seeing this.

How do you respond to your life with its seeming ups and downs? Is this present moment good enough for you? Are you attentive to life and patient enough with it so you can see the light behind the shadow, the sacred fire in the darkest experiences? Can you see your life is just perfect because at a profound level you chose to create it just as it is right now? If you created a shadow, it was in order to better see your light in contrast to it.

Our humanity does not interfere with our divinity; in fact, its contrast makes our divinity all the clearer.

Do you see love's hand in everything? *God is an all or nothing principle;* everything is pure Spirit. God is *the* Everything. How then can anything be called imperfect? If we say that something isn't good, we are saying that something isn't God. This, we know, is impossible.

But what about letting others starve? What about children who are pushed into prostituting for others' gain? How can we see perfection in light of the suffering all around us?

First, we must understand that things are not what they seem. We are always asked to see beyond the physical realm. For we don't know why certain things happen in life, what previous actions allowed them, or what might be their long term results. Only this can be said with certainty: all things have a purpose to the soul. Certain hardships make us stronger. Sometimes a person's life that we see as pitiful is here to remind us to be grateful. Often it appears others suffer to teach a lesson to those around them. Within the context of our human existence, we cannot know the reasons for such—and we do not need to. We need only decide what meaning something has for us in this moment. Does apparent pain in life trigger compassion in us or fear? And what do we choose to do about it? How are we going to use this to grow? This is what is far more important than the appearance itself.

If everything is ultimately good, does that include the ego too? Yes. In the wisdom of the One Self, we created the ego as a foil to our true Self to serve in and ensure our spiritual awakening. To fight the ego is therefore to fight a current aspect of self. Do not fight it. Witness it at work. See it for what it is—and go beyond it by dropping identification with it. Accept—yes, even love—the ego for playing so well, so convincingly the role we cast it in. Then discard it like a worn out garment that is of no more use to you.

M artin Buber, Jewish philosopher and theologian, told us there is *nothing* that cannot be made sacred. Indeed, there is nothing that is not *already* sacred. The perfection lies in correct perception. We heal all things through our very acceptance of them as divine. Problems cease to exist if we do not see them as problems. Can this perception include a broken leg? It can, if by seeing the broken leg as divine we see the hidden gift in it. If we see there is no mistake or problem in a broken leg, just an unexpected event, an unexpected form of perfection, we open ourselves to seeing that within the whole, within the One Self, everything is in its right place. This true forgiveness and deep healing does not un-break or mend the leg—it means we no longer need it to.

What we often call misfortunes are just times when the perfection of life comes in an unexpected, undesirable way. Why judge red as bad when you wanted green, or feel sad that what you sought did not arrive? We have all experienced a disappointment only to see that it was a necessary prelude to something wonderful: expected house guests call to say they can't come to stay this weekend after all; then, shortly afterward you hear your best friend is coming to town, and now you can invite her to stay with you; you lose your key only to find in your search the diamond ring you lost a year ago; a date cancels on you but you go to the party anyway, where you meet the love of your life; your husband leaves you, but because of this you find your own inner strength. Such evidence of perfection abounds.

What do we call a "mistake" if it is perfect? An opportunity, that's all. An opportunity to notice judgment and to forgive. Forgiveness is simply seeing perfection where you thought it wasn't. When we judge something or someone we see them as less than perfect. And because we are connected, the result is that we see ourselves as less than perfect. With every little announcement to ourselves of better and worse, we reinforce our own guilt. Yet in the reality of the soul there is only innocence.

Who or what do we judge as perfect? God. But judging also reaffirms our belief that we are separate from God. God is indeed perfect, but God is all that is—this includes you and your irritating neighbor down the street, the sun and the rain, a broken leg and a robust body. We can learn to be grateful for the spilled paint, to bless the seeming shortcomings of our social structure, to be calm with our children's difficulties. We show and give our love to God by loving ourselves. We love ourselves by loving the world just the way it is.

Appreciation is active acceptance of what is. It cancels all judgment. To appreciate our experiences is to know them as fundamentally good, divine. If you observe and appreciate even your judgments, you cancel their effects. A spiritual master makes mistakes too, but doesn't judge them as negative. To the master, every mistake is simply a point of learning, a step forward.

10

All things connect in the middle. It is here that they become one. It is at the middle that opposites unite, extremes are balanced, differences are reconciled, and conflicts are resolved. The path to the Middle Way is a sacred path, for it leads to our center. It is in the middle, at the center of our being, where we hold the value of everything with equal respect. Bias, prejudice, judgments of right and wrong, cannot exist in the center of our being. Here we find no opposites between good and bad, male and female, hot and cold. Instead, we realize that hot and cold are simply gradations of temperature, male and female are complementary aspects of ourselves, and good and bad are just different perspectives. Likewise, there is no you and me, only different expressions of the One.

E quanimity is key to transcending duality. And an accepting, impartial heart is the birthplace of peace. To express this in metaphor, it is at the center of the wheel of life that we find the greatest stillness and balance. The center of the wheel does not judge the individual spokes that revolve around it. The spokes are recognized as simply different expressions of our center, emanating from the One Self. The person currently opposite us on the wheel is a mirror reflection. And all the others who join the One Self in the middle are different images, different facets of our One Self. Each one is needed to create the perfect balance we find at the middle. The axle is the joining point; it supports and holds together the revolving spokes but is never itself changed by them.

It is impossible for the thinking mind to grasp the essence of the middle way. We must look with our heart. When we are faced with a choice, the middle way chooses all. It comes from inclusiveness, not preference.

Of course this does not mean that we do not make practical choices in our lives. We do, yet those choices are not made from a place of personal desire, but by embracing all options and moving in the highest direction of the moment.

When we can choose to reside in the middle, we are simultaneously connected to, yet detached from, the whirling world. We are in this world but not of it. We choose to move our attention away from residing on the rim of the wheel of life, running continuously through changing terrains, to its center where we experience stability and calm. We intuitively know that in challenging times we need to "get centered," to gather ourselves back from the superficial borders of life and connect again to our soul—the essence of our being.

The wheel of life is always in motion, going through different fields—snow and grass, manure and daisies. If we identify solely with the edges of the wheel, always interfacing variously with happiness or sadness, always anxiously reaching and racing toward the next thing, how can we be at peace? At the surface of the wheel, ups and downs with accompanying insecurities are experienced, but at the center we find stability.

So let us choose to reside at the center of the wheel of life, watching life's events spin around us, embracing it all by supporting, loving, accepting, being connected yet detached from the "drama," being creative yet not controlling. It is in the center of our being that we meet the One Self. It is here we see we are not different, not separate from each other. It takes all of us; it takes the One Self to form the center. The center is where we, as infinite "spokes" of the One consciousness, find community.

Here we find Self-love.

Here nothing is wrong.

And no thing is without value.

Apathy does not exist at the center of the wheel of life. What we find is compassionate detachment. Our heart center continuously extends itself through positive intent and action. A person like this is not idle, just not attached to outcomes. Detached from form, they are deeply connected. Realizing our Oneness, the master still chooses to make a difference in the lives of others. They are simultaneously fixed and grounded while extending their hands to the very edge of the wheel to support it and help ease its pressure.

11

May I love my beloved as God. May I love each person as my beloved. May I love the whole world as God. May I love the whole world as my beloved.

Most of mankind has been under the delusion that there are many kinds of love, each different in some way from the others. We talk of parental love, romantic love, platonic love, love of neighbor, love of God. Yet these are but different expressions of the same love moving through us. It is the same love that flows out of our being. It is the same heart that receives. In the end, it is just God loving another part of Itself.

A sacred partnership is not an end in itself. It is meant to liberate—not limit—our love. It is sacred because it provides a human vehicle for the experience and expansion of love.

Although we naturally become closer to a beloved as we expand spiritually, the primary purpose of human love is to grow ever closer to our essential, unlimited Self. A relation-*ship* can be likened to a transport vessel. The vessel is simply the means of connecting the two shores. The boat itself is useful, but it is not the point of the journey.

Intimacy with another is to help us grow beyond our own current perceptions of where love can and cannot exist. To love one person exclusively is not the heart's goal. Indeed, we cannot grow in authentic love for one person without growing in love for all of humanity. The heart's true nature is unconditional love for all.

The sacred connection of hearts goes beyond sex and the emotional fervor associated with what we have come to call romantic love with its needs and clinging born of insecurity. We are here to learn how to express love for all persons and things, not to focus it solely upon one or several objects of our affection.

We don't need to search desperately for a soul mate, life partner, or twin flame. We are not missing any parts, and no *body* can offer fulfillment. Love is already complete within itself. Love sees its beloved in every person. Love's very nature is to embrace others. Love cannot be confined. It consumes; it takes in all it touches; it burns away all separation, leaving only Oneness. When you truly love someone, that love expands to include the many and eventually to include all that is. You are Spirit. Can Spirit love only one person? Only several? Only a few hundred?

Although love transcends the personal, this does not mean you will not have one special relationship, preferring the company of one above others. And when your love expands, it does not mean that you don't love your partner. Do not confuse sexual exclusivity or monogamy with spiritual intimacy. They may or may not go hand in hand. They may be part of a love relationship—or not. A celibate monk could be your most intimate friend and your sexual partner like a remote stranger.

Although a partner is not necessary for spiritual growth, a partner can be of great assistance in this process. Your beloved can serve as your mirror, for they will not hesitate—out of unconditional love—to show you the things they see and you do not: your weaknesses, contradictions, blind spots, projections, and denials. Their teaching may come in the form of loving guidance, suggestion, feedback, bold action, and even confrontation. Consciously or not, they will invite you to open up the areas where you are withholding love.

True love flourishes, not because the individuals in the relationship are perfect or because the two are "ideally matched." It flourishes because the individuals have built their relationship on the adoration of love itself.

Relationships are sacred mirrors. In authentic love relationships, the partners mirror love to one another, and by this means come to see they are both reflections of the same Divine Light.

You have a relationship with your mother, your neighbor, your cat, and your shoes. You are in relationship with your car, the sun, the sea, your coffee mug, with Sam and his brother. What do these mirrors reflect back to you?

You exist in relation to others. Indeed, if there were no relationships, what is called a separate "you" would cease to exist. All that would remain would be Oneness—which is God. Ironically, this is exactly the purpose and destination of every relationship: to lead us to the awareness of unity, to the awareness of the One Self. When you feel you have merged with another person, you have effectively transcended duality. In this way, our friend, lover, or confidante can be our gateway to God. For we come to see that it is not the persona of the beloved that we merge with, but the non-personal Oneness— the I Am.

One thing that truly matters is this: are you expressing love right now? Love legitimizes all. When you love, you declare your true nature.

The fabric of your very existence, the substance of your soul, the stuff of atoms and of the entire cosmos is love. Yes, love helps you on your human journey. Yes, love brings harmony to your relationships. But most importantly, love expresses who you really are. When you love, you live as God—you live God into our world.

We have to own and bring to love all facets of our One Self. That which we call dark and negative is part of God too. If we do not see all as an expression of the One, if we put some in a category by themselves (terrorists, thieves, priests) we foster separation, making it more difficult for us and for them to transform.

The correct way to see any attack is as a call for inclusion and love from an individual who feels separate, and therefore afraid and wanting. Our most appropriate response is only one of love, which guarantees that it will be most appropriate to the situation and those involved. Our loving response may take any form, even a surprising one.

Open your self to love and compassion—and only then act. Every situation is different. Your love may take a passive or an active form. It may appear weak or strong, loud or soft. Don't let thoughts get in the way too much; just trust your heart, and do whatever love seems to ask of you in this moment. What would love do? This is the important question to ask.

You don't need to nor can you ever *get* love. You only need to express it. It is your very nature. It is not real love when you give in order to receive something or to accumulate good karma. It is real when it is from heart and not head, when it has no lid or limit. Only in this way do you come to know your true self—beyond the limitation of form and more encompassing than anything you can think or imagine you are. Love *moves* us. Only steps taken in love move us forward. All else is but a stationary dance. We get many opportunities, perhaps even many lifetimes, to learn to love unconditionally—to express the Self that we are. We are here to learn how to fully love every experience, every thing, every person, and every moment fully.

Let our prayer be for immediate intimacy. May we be able to feel our Oneness and the reality of our love essence in every moment, with every person, every thing, every experience.

Immediate Intimacy involves embracing every person, situation, and experience without the weight of our conditioned past, our personal baggage. It means setting judgments aside and relating to others without fear, without the need to be stronger or better than others or to control the encounter. It means meeting another and whatever the present moment brings without needs or limitations of any kind.

Let us be open, vulnerable, and unconditionally accepting of every part of the One Self. Let us greet everyone and everything with a willingness to love in whatever way feels highest. That is how we express our God Self on earth. It is our reason for human existence.

If we cannot greet another with authentic openness, we limit the love that can be expressed. If we cannot be intimate with the many forms of our One Self, we cannot know our many faces. Let us be open to loving the stranger with the same intensity and delight we would have when meeting our long-lost brother, for he *is* our long-lost brother. Lost because we thought he was a stranger, found because we now remember our connectedness.

The eyes are a wonderful avenue to experiencing immediate intimacy. They can express authentic love more clearly than any words. Eye to eye, you can suddenly be intimate with a stranger. Eye to eye, your masks fall away. Eye to eye, your "I" meets their "I". When you look, truly look deeply into the eyes of another, you see your Self looking back at you. In authentic encounter, you are as one presence.

Love is not a limited commodity, so why open the floodgate of your love for just one or a few people when you can open it to all? We start by loving another, then move to living intimately with all that is. The practice of intimacy is so holy because it is how we practice living as God. We become intimate with all that is. Is there something beyond being intimate with God? Yes, complete unity. It is here where relationships dissolve into the nameless One. The many have then again become One. The separation is healed.

It is true that you cannot love yourself fully until you love all things fully. For everything is a part of you, everything is a projection of the Self, everything is one in spirit. To love the neighbor is to love the self; to love the self is to love God.

12

To be the Christ is simply to be awakened to our divinity and to live it fully in the world. The ancient term for this is avatar. Historically, there have been very few avatars on earth. But exponentially, more and more are coming all the time. It seems that in this current age, the planet is ready for a whole portion of humanity to live their divinity in human form. As many more now start living their divinity, it will be increasingly difficult for others to ascribe their holiness to an outside God rather than the God who resides within.

There are no restrictions on who can awaken to their divine nature. If you are reading this now, you are surely part of this potential collective.

To live from our divine nature does not mean that we give up our humanity. Jesus and the Buddha knew well the sorrows of the world. Their compassion was great because their love of humanity was also deep.

In this time, we will not only predictably witness spiritual awakening on a larger—perhaps even a mass—scale, but will likely see more females awaken spiritually out of the need to bring into balance the male-female energy polarities. More important, perhaps, is that often the new avatars will no longer be just a single person, but a pair. They will not need to be cloistered nuns, lonely hermits, or chaste gurus. Many a new avatar will be couples who live very normal, very human lives and who together embody a single unit of balance and wholeness. Jesus and his beloved Mary Magdalene were the harbingers of the divine couples in our current age. They shone as one, as the embodiment of Love, yet only He was seen. We were not yet ready at that time to see Her, to see Them. Jesus and Mary knew and accepted this. They knew they were preparing the way. It is their legacy and lineage we are now fulfilling.

There was a time in humanity's history when females held the most power and influence. Later the power shifted to men. Now, we are healing the male-female polarity, healing this separation in the move to our Oneness. Neither male nor female will need to live in the shadow of the other. The power in their oneness will be visible.

13

God's domain is right here, right now. Everything exists in reality and potential in the now.

The present moment does not move. The movement of time is what is illusory. In this context, time is best understood as being vertical, not horizontal, holding every potential simultaneously in the now, awaiting our decision as to what we want to experience. Any belief that we cannot experience something is the mind's limitation, not of the One Self. And we can choose to experience the same things as many times as we wish.

All is right Now.
Right Now is All.
Now is All Right.
God is, and we are, All Right Now.

When we live as the One Self in this perpetual now moment, we dispel the illusion of space and time, and therefore of separation. It takes no time to do this. "It has taken time to misguide you so completely, but it takes no time at all to be what you are."[3] Our One Self exists now and awaits only our decision to experience it. To the linear thinking mind, the explosion of creation into unlimited forms and the re-union with source has already taken millions of years and still requires more time. It must be God's choice to delve into that explosion so every possible facet of the One Self can be appreciated, savored, and glorified.

As God, we choose to experience the intricacies of every snowflake that falls and the beauty of every sunrise. We choose to explore and relish every part of us—every flutter of every wing, every grain of sand, every human life—through all of eternity. We even choose to experience our dark side, to experience ourselves cut off from Self, devoid of love and hope.

[3] *A Course in Miracles*, Text, Chapter 15, 282

We want to miss nothing. That is why we created the illusion of time, for it allows us to enter the unlimited now and explore the One Self—even in the illusion of separation—for as long as we choose.

Can you imagine how incredible it would be if you could shrink and divide yourself so you could see and feel every cell and every atom in your body? Imagine experiencing just one moment of every aspect of your biology. After such an experience, how much more would you appreciate the unfathomable glory of doing this for one whole day?

In this context, each person can be likened to a cell of God's body, being experienced and appreciated by the entire mind of God. We experience life in this apparent stream of time, although all has actually taken no more than an instant in the mind of the One. This we do to appreciate our One Self fully and bring the love that we are to each and every aspect of our Self. In this way, the One experiences the beauty of the many so that the many can experience the glory of the One.

It is right now when the diversity can collapse into simple unity, where past and future can become meaningless and effort absurd. We can right now exist as pure awareness, knowing there is only the now and there is only one life. You may already have a glimpse of this reality—when time stops and your sense perception expands. It is then when you can feel your leaves brushing against your branches and feel the wind rush through your feathers. In this way, suddenly you *are* the abused wife, you *are* that beggar, that maimed soldier, that starving infant. It is then when you experience the "other" as the "self." Any time this happens, this connection sings to you of a point beyond judgment and duality, and this brings clarity. In this space of connection, what needs to be done next is easy, spontaneous, and healing.

We can invite this experience into our lives by living as if we already know we are one with all, right now. Each of us has likely had this experience, but how can we sustain it? To have something permanently, we must choose it perpetually.

Be Us Now.
Now—Us.
One moment, one Being.
Be the One Moment.
Be the One Self.
Be the one Now.
Be the One, now.
Every moment embodies eternity, just as every person embodies God.

Freedom does not come from teleporting, manifesting out of thin air, or flying. Neither is it acquired by having extensive knowledge of the spiritual realms. It comes by living detached from the cares, worries, and fears of this world. It comes by recognizing that who you truly are, has nothing to do with this form. Simply allowing things to be will reveal the inherent divinity in all of life. So will consciously letting go of fears and surrendering to the effortless flow of life in unplanned and non-judgmental living within the present moment. We need to take the risk of being vulnerable, of dropping our defenses, to experience the truth of our Being. We need to risk opening to the perfection, to the loving benevolence of the Oneness.

The human race has accumulated much mind knowledge, yet pain, conflict, and violence still prevail. What use is our knowledge if the innocent child, ignorant of the world, is closer to heaven than the most erudite scholar or priest? Learning more will not set us free from the limitations and travails of life.

We deceive ourselves by thinking we need to *know* more, *do* more, in order to live joyfully. This has been our excuse for maintaining our masks, pretensions, and safeguards, and for denying that it is our own personal refusal to experience bliss that keeps it from us. Every limitation is self-imposed.

The truth *will* set you free, but first *you* must set free the truth.

When we stop working so hard to maintain the illusion of our separation, the reality of the One Self will be obvious. The One Self is who we are as soon as we stop pretending to be otherwise. When the mind asks, "What is God?" the heart points to whatever is present and says, "This." God is what *Is*. "I Am that I Am." God is not out there, but in us and around us.

It is not with the mind but with the eyes of innocence that we become aware of this truth. The One Self cannot be grasped by thought. Thought, by its very nature, isolates one thing from the whole, breaks it off, so to speak, and therefore it must be false or a distortion at best. If we are still struggling spiritually by trying to find out more, may our prayer be that we come to "learn" enough so we can understand that all our learning was not only unnecessary for spiritual awareness, but also an obstacle to our awakening. May spiritual truth be born out of the ashes of our knowledge.

14

We do not need the external world to change before we can find peace. We need only bring love to it. Life is love. Love is life. We start one when we choose the other. We cannot leave what we cannot love, for finding love wherever we are is exactly the reason we are here. And we don't want to leave this earth party until we get our gift.

How can we experience the benevolence of the universe unless we trust ourselves and one another? Unless we trust God? Our security cannot be found in the outer world, in anything or anyone outside of ourselves—this includes a detached, outside God. The peace that comes with knowing that we live in a universe of our choosing, and all is well, is available to us now. The peace of God comes from knowing that we are all pieces of God.

Living As God | 123

Jesus was no more intrinsically holy than the thieves who died beside him. He differed from them, however, in his knowing that "I and the Father are One." Knowing we are all One with the Father, how *could* He judge "others?" He knew that God was equally present in everyone and had enormous compassion for those who had forgotten this. Until we remember this, we cannot know what we do to each other or to our world.

We are as important to God as God is to us. Through us does the One come to know Itself in form. Through us, God's experience of Itself is made complete. We are God experienced and expressed.

We are the Living God.

Living is being God.

God is living you.

Your life is God, being.

The kingdom is at hand, for it is in *our* hands now. *It is within us.*

To acknowledge and celebrate the One Self is our purpose. It is what we are called to do. When we appreciate every person, thing, experience, as an expression of the One Self, we abide in joy and peace, the natural state of our soul. What effort, what defenses or grievances, are necessary when we abide in the safety of our unity? All needs dissolve; only grace remains.

We don't need to grasp for air; we simply need to breathe. Similarly, there is no need to grasp for God, who is our deepest, truest Self. It is by our awareness of this that we enter into a whole new dimension of peace. Let us abide in and act from this realization.

This book can never end, for in you it now lives forever. And forever our love will expand.

As every ending is a beginning, let us begin.

The name Rob McRae is simply a temporary label. It and the person it points to have no inherent meaning. It could be any name—Chris, Raymond, Pauline, or your name, if you like. Every name belongs to both you and me, for we are each part of everyone. The heart that speaks here is the same one that is deep within you and everyone else. Also, the physical identity of the person who birthed this book does not matter. It is truly irrelevant whether a man or a woman, a Caucasian or an Asian, a scholar or a priest put this to paper. All that matters—about this book and about everything—is that it *is*.

Be willing to suspend your belief that a single author wrote this. Instead, be open to the possibility, to the realization that we all are One, and therefore it has taken the agreement of the whole universe to get this book into your hands. This, like any book or any thing, is the perfect expression of one part of us, with the agreement of and for the benefit of the other parts of us.

We all agreed that this book be written. And here it is.